AL-BIRUNI

Master Astronomer and
Muslim Scholar of the Eleventh Century

Great Muslim Philosophers and Scientists of the Middle Ages™

AL-BIRUNI

Master Astronomer and
Muslim Scholar of the Eleventh Century

Bill Scheppler

The Rosen Publishing Group, Inc., New York

Published in 2006 by The Rosen Publishing Group, Inc.
29 East 21st Street, New York, NY 10010

First Edition

Library of Congress Cataloging-in-Publication Data

Scheppler, Bill.
Al-Biruni: master astronomer and Muslim scholar of the eleventh century/Bill Scheppler—1st ed.
    p. cm.—(Great Muslim philosophers and scientists of the Middle Ages)
Includes bibliographical references and index.
ISBN 1-4042-0512-8 (library binding)
1. Biruni, Muhammad ibn Ahmad, 973?–1048. 2. Scientists—Uzbekistan—Biography. 3. Scientists—Iran—Biography. 4. Muslim scientists—Uzbekistan—Biography. 5. Muslim scientists—Iran—Biography. 6. Science—Middle East—History—To 1500. 7. Islam and science—History—To 1500.
I. Title. II. Series.
Q143.B5S35 2006
509'.2—dc22

                                                    2005012236

Manufactured in the United States of America

On the cover: This portrait of al-Biruni appeared on a stamp that was issued in the Soviet Union in 1973, 1,000 years after al-Biruni's birth.

CONTENTS

Introduction

FOCUS ON MUSLIM LANDS

At the turn of the first millennium, the eyes of the educated world were focused on Muslim lands, particularly what is now called the Middle East. By the end of the tenth century, the writings of Greek philosophers, such as Aristotle, Plato, and Hippocrates, had been widely translated, distributed, and studied, and a new era of discovery was under way. Muslim scholars, once content to gain knowledge through reading the works of past masters, began to apply new thinking to age-old theories.

Persian historian Rashid al-Din wrote a history of the Mongol rulers entitled *Compendium of Chronicles* (circa 1295–1310) for Ghazan Khan. An enthroned Mongolian ruler in Iran is pictured here, surrounded by members of his court. Many rulers in Muslim lands supported the intellectual pursuits of scholars at their royal courts.

Inspired by their faith, Islam, these men believed they could become closer to God (in Arabic, Allah), by understanding his creations. Abu Raihan al-Biruni and his contemporaries challenged the conventional wisdom and conducted independent experiments to draw their own conclusions—many of which proved existing theories incorrect. This quest for truth permeated the Muslim civilization, motivating scholars to seek knowledge through research and innovation.

After early scholarly efforts under the Umayyad and Abbasid rulers, the evolution of numerous independent dynasties throughout the Muslim lands gave rise to wealthy regional sultans who collected knowledge as riches. They built opulent libraries, filling the shelves with the most celebrated volumes of the day, and invited renowned scholars to study under their patronage, paving the way for full-time academics. Sultans took care of all earthly needs for the Muslim scholars who studied in their courts. This carefree living situation enabled scholars to devote their lives to learning and to make significant advancements in their fields of study. Scholars typically dedicated new books and treatises to the sultans in recognition of their patronage, and the sultans reveled in the status of being associated with pioneering academic works. The combination of passionate academic pursuit and high regard for knowledge set the stage for a period of remarkable intellectual enlightenment, during which Muslim lands from Spain in the west to India in the East outpaced the rest of the world for the next several hundred years.

At the turn of the second millennium, the eyes of the educated world were once again focused on the Middle East—this time for all the wrong reasons. Once the world's leading region in wealth, culture, and literature, the Middle East became largely associated with terrorism, war, and oil reserves. And when seen through the lens of Western media, one-time centers of education and commerce such as Afghanistan and Iraq come across as little more than war-torn, third-world countries. In the twenty-first century, we seem to remember little about the magnificent history of the Middle East and the myriad scientific advancements Muslim scholars achieved during the so-called Middle Ages (the European name for the period of European history from AD 500 to about 1500). This extraordinary era was all but replaced in Western history books by the Renaissance, Europe's period of enlightenment, which commenced at the turn of the fifteenth century, building largely on the prior achievements of Muslim civilization.

The names and works of Renaissance scholars such as Leonardo da Vinci and Galileo Galilei are well known throughout the Western world—and deservedly so. But in order to appreciate fully the origin and advancement of arts and sciences, we must expand our historical perspective to study those who came before and paved the way for future scientific discovery. Mathematic disciplines such as algebra and

This map depicts the ruling dynasties and their territories around AD 1000. Al-Biruni was born in 973 in Khwarizm, the area of present-day Khiva, Uzbekistan, which lies south of the Aral Sea.

trigonometry, for example, are fundamental to accurate calculations in the field of astronomy. Both disciplines originated in Muslim lands, yet we know more about the Renaissance scholars who applied the formulas than the Muslim scholars who developed them. The time is ripe to increase our understanding of this pivotal region of the globe.

Although Muslims throughout the lands of Islam shared a keen desire to acquire knowledge, a handful of men emerged

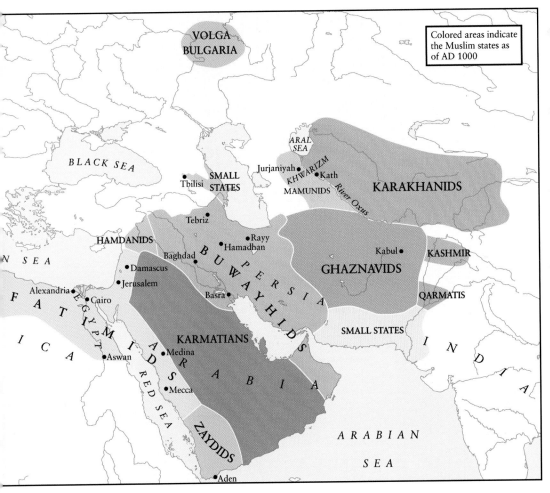

as the greatest scholars of their time and justifiably some of the greatest minds in history. Abu Raihan al-Biruni set himself apart from his peers through his sheer range of expertise and drive for perfection. His considerable progress in astronomy, mathematics, geography, comparative religion, physical sciences, and history earned the respect of his colleagues, influenced countless academic followers, and remains as an inspiration to all who study his work today.

Chapter 1

THE RISE AND SPREAD OF ISLAM

According to Islamic teaching, in the year AD 610, the angel Gabriel is said to have appeared to Muhammad, an Arab trader and businessman, as he meditated alone inside a cave on Mount Hira. From his mountain refuge that overlooked Mecca (Makkah), Muhammad, initially reluctant, accepted Gabriel's call to become a prophet of God. This event marked the genesis of the religion of Islam. By the tenth century, Islam was more than 400

This miniature of the angel Gabriel is from a copy of *The Wonders of Creation and the Oddities of Existence* that dates from 1375 to 1425. Zakariya Qazwini, a judge who lived in Wasit, Iraq, compiled the original book in 1270. It deals with the marvels of the universe in the fields of geography, astronomy, astrology, and natural history.

و مِنْهُمْ جَبْرَئِيلُ

فَإِذَا بَلَغَ أَمِيرُ الْوَحْيِ وَخَازِنُ الْقُدُسِ وَيُقَالُ لَهُ أَيْضًا الرُّوحُ الْأَمِينُ وَالرُّوحُ الْقُدُسُ
وَالنَّامُوسُ الْأَكْبَرُ وَطَاوُسُ الْمَلَائِكَةِ   جَاءَهُ لِلْخِزَانِ أَنَّ اللَّهَ تَعَالَى إِذَا أَنْكُمْ بِالَّذِي
سَمِعَ أَهْلُ السَّمَاءِ صَلْصَلَةً كَجَرِّ السِّلْسِلَةِ عَلَى الصَّفَا فَيُصْعَقُونَ وَلَا يَزَالُونَ كَذَلِكَ
حَتَّى تَأْتِيهِمْ جَبْرَئِيلُ فَإِذَا جَاءَهُمْ فُزِّعَ عَنْ قُلُوبِهِمْ فَقَالُوا يَا جَبْرَئِيلُ مَاذَا قَالَ رَبُّكَ
فَيَقُولُ الْحَقَّ فَأَدَّنَ مِنَ الْحَقِّ   وَجَاءَ بِالْجِنَانِ النَّبِيَّ صَلَّى اللَّهُ عَلَيْهِ وَآلِهِ وَسَلَّمَ
قَالَ لِجَبْرَئِيلَ إِنِّي أُحِبُّ أَنْ أَرَاكَ عَلَى صُورَتِكَ فَقَالَ إِنَّكَ لَا تُطِيقُ ذَلِكَ قَالَ

years old and had spread throughout the Middle East and beyond, although many inhabitants of these lands continued to practice other religions. A political leader known as the caliph, which literally means "successor to the prophet," was located in the city of Baghdad in the heart of Persia. By this time, followers of Islam, called Muslims, could be found as far east as the Indian border, north into Turkey, south to the upper regions of Africa, and as far west as al-Andalus, which was located in present-day Spain. This widespread expansion of Muslim lands exposed Muslims to new cultures, religions, and learning, creating an environment in which scholars were challenged to sift through the abundance of knowledge and separate fact from fiction.

For a variety of reasons, Muslim scholars during the Middle Ages were in a unique position to conduct in-depth research, evaluate and test conflicting theories, and share their conclusions with the rest of the educated world. The expansion of Muslim territory over a huge geographic region strained the political influence of the caliphate, which is the government ruled by the caliph. As a result, independent dynasties emerged to rule over various subregions of Muslim territory. These dynasties developed centers of learning away from Baghdad, therefore increasing the overall number of Muslim scholars. At the same time, the rulers, often referred to as sultans, continued to look to the caliph to acknowledge their rule. The caliph's continued influence preserved centralization across the region, and as Muslim civilization developed, a common language (Arabic) and economy played a key role in enabling scholars to communicate and travel between regions. In addition, Muslim scholars devoted their work to Islam, which is firmly rooted in the philosophy of *al-tawhid*, an Arabic term meaning divine unity among all beings. This ideology—which teaches that the more a man learns, the closer he comes to knowing universal truth and understanding God—compelled Muslim scholars to study diverse information with fervor. In his book *A History of India (Tarikh al-Hind)*, al-Biruni defined this philosophy as "striving to become as much as possible similar to God." He exemplified al-tawhid as well or better than any other scholar in history, studying everything from the rocks under his feet to the farthest known planets in the heavens, all in the name of God.

THE FORMATION OF INDEPENDENT DYNASTIES

The caliphate began its decline in the mid-ninth century during the reign of Caliph al-Mutawakkil, who was murdered in AD 861 and succeeded by his brother Caliph al-Wathiq. This weakening of central power led to the rise of independent dynasties, particularly in the Muslim lands that were farthest from the caliph's contact. Regional military leaders rose to prominence through battle, alliance, and succession. They

This silver medallion is stamped with the portrait of al-Mutawakkil (822–861), who was caliph of the Abbasid dynasty in Samarra (Iraq) and ruler of the Muslim world. Nearly thirty years after his death, the Abbasid capital was moved back to Baghdad.

established kingdoms and paid only token allegiance to the caliph. The diminished political leadership of the caliphate led to increased bloodshed among Muslim groups vying for power. Political fragmentation was accompanied by religious tension between Sunni, Shiite, and other sects. Yet the chaos did not damage the cultural and literary unity of Muslim civilization—in fact, culture flourished. The court culture of Baghdad was emulated in each region, and Muslims began studying additional subjects in more places with exposure to new influences.

By the tenth century, Muslim dynasties with names such as Samanid, Mamunid, and Ghaznavid were well established. Many of these rulers recognized knowledge as a symbol of affluence and actually competed with one another to build the most impressive libraries and bring prominent scholars into their courts. When the caliphate was strong, the empire's provinces were required to submit

This fifteenth-century Arabic copy of a manuscript entitled *Advantages Derived from Animals* (circa 1300) is based on the writings of the Greek philosopher Aristotle. Some of the riches amassed by regional rulers in Muslim territories were used to commission scholars to research, translate, or write on scientific and philosophical works from ancient cultures, such as the Greek, Roman, and Indian cultures.

surplus wealth to the treasury of the caliph. However, with the decline of the caliphate, regional rulers held on to this wealth and began to amass considerable riches. The regional rulers used this increased wealth to purchase the greatest books for their libraries or to pay the most celebrated intellectuals to work under their patronage. The rulers' patronage provided scholars with the financial security to study full-time, sometimes awarding massive amounts of silver and other gifts for undertaking significant works, a practice later found in cities such as Florence and Venice during the Renaissance. But the academic riches were not reserved only for sultans and scholars—they truly served to expand the collective Muslim intellect.

Wealthy citizens began to emulate their sultans' desires to collect books. This trend fed not only the business of transcribing texts, as demand grew for multiple copies of renowned works, but also the culture of learning. The increased availability of paper and books enabled students to vastly improve their education without the need to travel to the origins of the subject matter. Study groups sprung up at mosques, the buildings where Muslims gather for daily prayer, and travelers had the opportunity to continue their studies while trekking from town to town. This quest for knowledge elevated the level of education for all Muslim citizens, developing a more sophisticated intellectual base and influencing future scholars.

COMMON LANGUAGE AND ECONOMY

The weakening of the caliphate benefited those Muslim sultans who obtained sovereignty to build independent dynasties, acquire regional power, and amass riches. But the overall strength of Muslim civilization remained a key ingredient in the continuing prosperity of the Middle East, and the caliph continued to be an important symbol for maintaining cultural and religious unity. Aside from the city of Baghdad, regions such as Khurasan and Transoxiana emerged as influential centers of learning. Although these regions were not under Abbasid rule, they did form part of the extensive Muslim lands, sharing a unified economy based on the gold dinar and the Arabic language. This stability fostered collaboration among scholars and Muslims in general. For example, books written in Transoxiana could be studied by Muslim students in Baghdad, academics working under the patronage of one dynasty could transfer to another, and scholars on research expeditions could travel just about anywhere without much difficulty.

Although the open communication that comes with any shared language is invaluable to the advancement of knowledge, it was the Arabic language in particular that enabled the Middle East to become the world's intellectual leader during the Middle Ages. Arabs spoke several languages and dialects, but Arabic emerged as the standard language adopted across the Muslim lands. As they researched various philosophies and sciences, Muslim scholars studied books written in Greek, Hebrew, Sanskrit, and other languages. Arabic was unique in that its alphabet was flexible enough to support the translation of texts in a variety of languages, yet specific enough to provide complete explanations of complex subjects such as mathematics and the natural sciences. Making these volumes available

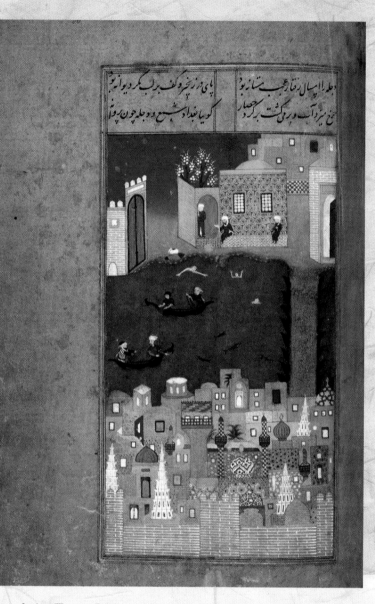

A view of the Tigris River in Baghdad is depicted in this miniature painting from a fifteenth-century manuscript by Nasir Bukhara'i. Baghdad's central location between Europe and the Far East helped to make the city a trade center and a gathering place for intellectuals.

uniformly in Arabic provided all Muslims with access to the most sophisticated information of the day.

The location of Baghdad, centrally positioned between Europe and the Far East, made it a mandatory stop on the world's most important medieval trade routes as merchants moved goods westward out of Asia. Baghdad became one of the richest cities of the era, and a shared currency across the caliphate facilitated the spread of wealth to other Muslim towns along the trade network. It was during this time that cities such as Tehran and Kabul emerged as major economic centers. The cultures of the East and the West came together in Baghdad and transformed the Muslim capital into a whirlwind of intellectual activity. As knowledge came into Muslim lands from outside cultures, Muslim scholars studied and evaluated it and recorded their conclusions. The resulting texts were swept up into the same westward trade routes, surfacing in al-Andalus and eventually throughout Europe. In this way, the works of Muslim scholars began to permeate and influence the rest of the educated world.

A CULTURE OF KNOWLEDGE AND TRUTH

The Islamic teaching concerning education and enlightenment is fairly unique among major religions in that it specifically encourages its followers to pursue knowledge. Muhammad himself called upon Muslims to make all efforts to learn, and the holy book of Islam, the Qur'an (Koran), asks believers to "observe, study, and draw conclusions." Although some Muslims insisted this call to knowledge was limited to the study of the Qur'an itself, many early Muslims interpreted it as a command to consume as much information as possible, as an act of faith within Islam. Muslim scholars viewed knowledge as a means to become closer to God. They believed that studying the world results in a more comprehensive understanding of God, the creator of all things, and is the responsibility of human beings as God's stewards on Earth. This drive for knowledge spanned the different economic and social classes, from powerful sultans down to ordinary citizens, and education became a vital part of Muslim existence and engagement with the world.

The mosque serves as the center of Islamic religious life. Following regular prayers, study groups began to meet regularly in the *maktab*, or office, attached to the mosque. This practice became so engrained in Muslim culture that today "maktab" is the Arabic word for "school." In major

The ceramic *mihrab*, or prayer niche, from the Maydan Mosque in Kashan, Iran, was constructed in 1226. The mihrab is the niche in the wall of a mosque that indicates the direction of the Kaaba, the small stone building in the courtyard of the Great Mosque in Mecca and the point toward which Muslims pray. The inscriptions contained on this mihrab are verses from the Qur'an.

cities, these early schools were influenced by the growth of libraries and an increase in the number of Muslim scholars. The schools evolved into centers of higher education that drew their curricula from secular as well as religious sources. Once again, Baghdad led the way, becoming one of the greatest centers of learning in history. Its citizens appreciated and studied literature, poetry, and fine arts.

As information about other countries and cultures became widely available, Muslims became more interested in travel. Travel presents opportunities for exchanging information, and learning from different people and cultures was regarded as an ideal method of broadening one's mind. In this spirit, sultans often encouraged scholars to embark on expeditions with the purpose of mapping a region and documenting their findings for the benefit of the court and its subjects. The brightest Muslim scholars were valued, respected, and often well compensated in this Muslim culture of knowledge. Such is the environment into which Abu Raihan al-Biruni rose to prominence.

Chapter 2

THE MAN AND HIS STUDIES

In AD 973, the area we know today as Khiva, Uzbekistan, was a relatively small but thriving cultural, economic, and literary center called Khwarizm. The kingdom of Khwarizm was divided into two parts, each one ruled by an independent dynasty. Abu Ali Mamun bin Muhammad ruled one half of Khwarizm from the city of Jurjaniyah, and the other half was ruled by Ahmad bin Muhammad bin Iraq from his capital city at Kath. On September 4, 973, Abu Raihan Muhammad ibn Ahmad al-Biruni was born on the outskirts of Kath. Little is known for certain about al-Biruni's upbringing because he was not from an

A stamp with al-Biruni's portrait was issued in Egypt in 1975, 980 years after the publication of al-Biruni's *Cartography*. Abu Raihan Muhammad ibn Ahmad al-Biruni was born on September 4, 973, near Kath in Khwarizm.

influential family and he left no autobiographical writings. But what we can glean from available sources is that al-Biruni was born to a Shiite Muslim family of modest means, originally from the country of Tajikistan in Central Asia, west of China. Al-Biruni, the genius scholar whose work has proved inspirational for a thousand years, was a self-made man. He built his great reputation and fame solely on the merits of his remarkable body of work.

Education was available to all Muslims in the tenth century, and al-Biruni excelled scholastically from a very young age. He had an analytical mind and was attracted to mathematics and astronomy early on, but he also employed the social insight of a historian and enjoyed studying cultures later in life. It is this rare intellectual dexterity that propelled al-Biruni into his place among the elite of history's great intellectuals. A devout Muslim, al-Biruni had a religious conviction that fueled his quest for knowledge, and he was as prolific as he was brilliant. All told, al-Biruni is credited with some 180 books. He wrote most of these himself; scholars under his direction penned the others. Living and working during a high point of Muslim civilization, he was consistently motivated and challenged by his mentors and contemporaries, many of whom were superior scholars in their own right. Al-Biruni never had a family of his own. He dedicated himself to the pursuit of knowledge and spent most of his life studying in the courts of sultans.

A DEVOTED MUSLIM FIRST AND FOREMOST

A celebrated scholar, al-Biruni was first and foremost a devoted Muslim. He held his religious beliefs very deeply and built his work around his faith. In the prevailing tone of spiritual unity, he tried to embrace both Shia and Sunni, the two main branches of Islam that clashed over the issue of Muhammad's rightful successor, and wore a ring on his finger with two identical stones symbolizing his reverence for each branch. As a Muslim scholar, al-Biruni became proficient in nearly every field of medieval learning as a means to seek greater truth in the name of Islam. He began his studies by examining existing theories of other scholars and philosophers and then sought to disprove any conclusions that went against the teachings of the Qur'an. Al-Biruni believed this virtuous objective should be held as the duty of all Muslim scholars.

In his book *The Chronology of Ancient Nations (Kitab al-Athar al-Baqiyah an al-qurun al-Khaliya)*, al-Biruni wrote, "Many people attribute to God's wisdom all they do not know of physical sciences." This statement was made in criticism of those who would dismiss an event rather than make the effort to determine its true natural cause. Al-Biruni believed that each time he discovered the answer to an unexplained phenomenon through reason and research, he further revealed God's relationship to humankind, ultimately bringing him closer to God. Al-Biruni viewed the path to understanding God as a methodical process. Answers inevitably lead to more questions, allowing the student to perceive complexity in things that might first appear simple. Consequently, they open a student's mind to the infinite nature of the Divine Creator. Under al-Biruni's philosophy, no area of study is outside the realm of God because he believed studying anything exposes a connection to everything in creation.

Al-Biruni approached the integration of science and religion in a logical manner. His drive to seek universal truth in God's universe fed a number of pioneering advancements and accurate discoveries, but there were times when al-Biruni's religious focus may have influenced his conclusions. For example: modern scientists believe Earth evolves gradually at a relatively imperceptible rate—with the exception of events such as earthquakes, volcanic eruptions, and floods, when we literally witness Earth changing form. Al-Biruni asserted that

"The Investiture of Ali at Ghadir Khumm" is illustrated in this 1307–1308 copy of al-Biruni's *The Chronology of Ancient Nations*. Some Muslims believe that while traveling across the plain of Ghadir Khumm, the prophet Muhammad, after receiving a revelation from God, proclaimed that Ali should be his successor. The Muslims who supported Ali as the successor became known as Shiites. The Sunnis believe that the successor to the Prophet must be a member of Muhammad's tribe, the Quraysh tribe. Al-Biruni, a pious Muslim, tried to embrace both branches of Islam and integrated his quest for knowledge in the sciences with his religious studies.

these large-scale disasters occur periodically when God intends to purify inhabited territories and to remind us that his hand never stops intervening in the world. However, when engaging in comparative religious study, al-Biruni learned to separate philosophy from his Muslim beliefs. This approach, inspired by *The Metaphysics* and other writings of Persian physician, philosopher, and alchemist Abu Bakr Muhammad ibn Zakariya al-Razi (865–925), enabled him to study differing religions objectively without constantly comparing them to Islam.

INFLUENTIAL SCHOLARS AND CONTEMPORARIES

Today, historians credit al-Biruni's aptitude for learning when he was a youth to his gifted mind and passion for knowledge, but they have little insight into his earliest influences. The first figure known to have played a key role in al-Biruni's educational development was the Persian mathematician and astronomer Abu Nasr Mansur ibn Iraq (970–1036). He was al-Biruni's mentor and an exceptional scholar, but he was also a prince of the Banu Iraq dynasty at Kath and al-Biruni's first patron. Abu Nasr Mansur ibn Iraq, in turn, was a student of Abu al-Wafa al-Buzjani (940–998), who developed geometrical problem-solving methods, and he was greatly influenced by mathematician and astronomer Muhammad al-Khwarizmi (780–850), who studied at the House of Wisdom, a well-known educational and reasearch institution located in Baghdad. Al-Khwarizmi, along with al-Farghani (circa 820–861), had been responsible for building the Khwarizm region's reputation as an influential center of mathematics. Expanding on al-Khwarizmi's works, Abu Nasr Mansur ibn Iraq made great strides in trigonometry and astronomy, including a formula known as the law of sines. Al-Biruni carried on in this tradition, and he would make the era's most significant contributions to these fields.

Al-Biruni studied and wrote on the teachings of many of his predecessors. He so respected the work of al-Razi (also known as Rhazes, the Latin form of his name) in the areas of medicine, physics, and philosophy that he also studied in depth the writings of al-Razi's teacher Iran Shahri, who wrote on the doctrines of Manichaeanism and other ancient religions. In the area of astronomy, he respected Abu Mashar and al-Battani. In mathematics, he also studied al-Khujandi. And he was quite familiar with philosophers such as al-Farabi and his successor Ibn Sina (980–1037), who was a contemporary of al-Biruni's. But al-Biruni never lost sight of the pursuit of truth. He regularly challenged his masters and mentors. Al-Biruni always conducted his own research and revised previously accepted conclusions when he found his calculations to be more accurate.

Al-Biruni and Ibn Sina (Avicenna in Latin) competed and collaborated with each other for most of their professional lives. The two scholars had great respect for each other and corresponded regularly, debating issues (such as the potential existence of a world different in nature from their own) they felt were beyond the intellect of other scholars of the day. But al-Biruni would never ask Ibn Sina about mathematics or astronomy, areas in which he believed he was the undisputed expert. He would, rather, pose questions about philosophy and physical sciences, subjects in which Ibn Sina excelled. However, even in these areas, al-Biruni challenged Ibn Sina's ideas. As with any other source, al-Biruni did not blindly accept Ibn Sina's answers; instead, he would often challenge his colleague and force debate. In a famous correspondence between the two, al-Biruni posed a series of questions to Ibn Sina, including one challenging Aristotle's claim that gravity does not affect the movement of celestial bodies. Ibn Sina answered all the questions only to have the majority of his responses denounced by al-Biruni. So dominant and influential were these two men that their works

This map of the Sea of Azov, showing the Black Sea in the top left corner, is an eleventh-century copy of one made by Muhammad al-Khwarizmi (780–850). Al-Biruni studied the works of al-Khwarizmi, who was a mathematician, geographer, and astronomer, and wrote about al-Khwarizmi's contributions in the sciences.

الحر

ديا فيقا

Al-Biruni Vs. Aristotle: Challenging Conventional Wisdom

Up until the late tenth century, most new knowledge in the Muslim lands was gathered through translation. Works of the great Greek scholars and philosophers were translated into Arabic and lined the shelves of libraries in the Muslim territories. Al-Biruni's predecessors had studied the works of the celebrated thinkers of the fourth and third centuries BC, such as Hippocrates, Plato, and Aristotle, and generally accepted their findings as fact. Consequently, Muslim science and philosophy were founded on the writings of Greek scholars. During al-Biruni's era, however, Muslims had caught up on past learning and began to *produce* and advance knowledge through experimentation and further research. Al-Biruni, too, studied Aristotle's works, but he spent a great deal of time challenging previously accepted conclusions and developing his own more accurate methods and theories. In this way, Aristotle may be looked upon as al-Biruni's greatest influence because his work motivated al-Biruni to question conventional wisdom in favor of his own findings, which he refined through Islamic teachings. Al-Biruni did not dismiss Aristotle entirely; in fact, he greatly respected the Greek philosopher as a man of learning and looked to his work as a resource. He did, however, criticize Aristotle's line of reasoning and scrutinize his methodology as he pushed wisdom to evolve closer to absolute truth.

In this Persian miniature, Iskandar (Alexander the Great), enthroned, meets seven sages (Aristotle, Apollonius, Socrates, Plato, Thales, Porphyrius, and Hermes). The illustration appears in poet Nezami's (1141–1203 or 1217) work entitled *Khamseh* (The Quintet), which contains five romantic epic poems. This scene is taken from a 1501 Arabic copy of the poem "Iskandar-Nama" (The Book of Alexander the Great), and acknowledges the importance of the ancient Greek philosophers to the scholars and writers living in Muslim lands from about 1000 to 1600.

alone encompass the basic elements and methods found in the writings of most Muslim academics that followed.

AL-BIRUNI'S REMARKABLE BODY OF WORK

Modern-day scholars credit al-Biruni with almost 200 written works. Of these works, relatively few remain—the vast majority were lost over the course of a thousand years.

Many of al-Biruni's existing volumes still have not been translated from Arabic, making it difficult for Western academics to study his complete body of work. Moreover, a comprehensive study has yet to be conducted. Al-Biruni was a man whose intellectual aptitude was as diverse as any of history's greatest thinkers, yet in the twenty-first century, researchers find themselves merely scratching the surface of this great scholar's vast knowledge and teachings.

Arguably, al-Biruni's greatest contributions to academia are his extensive advancements in astronomy and his books *The Chronology of Ancient Nations*, written around AD 1000, and *A History of India (Tarikh al-Hind)*, completed in 1030. Chapter 6 of this book is dedicated to al-Biruni's work in astronomy, and chapter 7 focuses on *The Chronology of Ancient Nations* and *A History of India* as two of his key writings. The remainder of this chapter touches on some of the other fields of study to which al-Biruni made significant contributions during his distinguished life of learning.

Mathematics

It is impossible to map and track the heavens without understanding mathematical equations and theory. Al-Biruni had to become expert in arithmetic, algebra, and geometry in order to begin to understand astronomy. His experiments to further the science of astronomy required

Some of al-Biruni's studies involving triangles are pictured in this illustration from a 1934 translation of his book entitled *Instruction in the Elements of the Art of Astrology* (1029). According to the English translation by R. Ramsay Wright, al-Biruni wrote: "The side of a triangle opposite a right or obtuse angle is the longest side, if it is a right angle, the hypotenuse. Of the other sides, if they are different, one is designated the shorter of the short sides, the other the longer of these."

that he develop advanced theories in mathematics as well. Different from words and language, numbers are truly universal, and al-Biruni's innovations in mathematics spread quickly across borders and cultures.

Al-Biruni's astronomy experiments, such as measuring the distances between Earth and celestial bodies, pushed the limits of mathematics because existing formulas were inadequate to accurately measure the sizes and distances of heavenly objects. He helped develop mathematics from geometry to trigonometry and finally to spherical trigonometry and calculus. In his book *Astronomy and Trigonometry (Al-Qanun al-Mas'udi)*, his ultimate contribution to trigonometry, al-Biruni presented previously unknown mathematical equations that he developed to measure the circumference of Earth and explain the planet's rotation on its axis. The book also defines methods for measuring the various sides of shapes up to the decagon and goes on to describe calculations of arcs and complementary arcs. He formulated techniques to find the radius of a circle, which are the first examples of calculus in classical mathematics. As in other areas of study, al-Biruni researched the methods of past scholars, such as Abu al-Wafa al-Buzjani and al-Khwarizmi, and critically evaluated their work to arrive at more accurate results.

During al-Biruni's extensive study of India and the culture of its people, he came across new concepts in mathematics, some of which were previously unknown outside Indian borders. He wrote no fewer than eight books on Indian arithmetic, introducing many of these concepts into Muslim lands and beyond for the first time. One example appears in his book *Zodiac in India (Rashikhat al-Hind)* in which al-Biruni describes an Indian numerical exercise as follows: with three numbers known, the student must ascertain the fourth in the series by understanding the relationship between the first two, projecting it upon the third, and using this formula to calculate the fourth.

Geography

Geography is another science that is inherently connected with astronomy because we learn about the composition of other celestial bodies by studying Earth. Al-Biruni excelled in this area as well. Al-Biruni accepted the ancient concept that the universe was made up of four basic elements: earth, water, air, and fire. He could, therefore, study Earth as a microcosm (small-scale model) of the entire universe and use his experiments to project universal theories. Another connection between astronomy and geographical studies was al-Biruni's use of celestial bodies in orbit above Earth as gauges to measure and record accurate positions of sites on Earth. Given the limited technology of his day, mastery of astronomy was essential to geographic studies.

Like other scholars of his era, al-Biruni was familiar with only about half of Earth's landmass—essentially, the continents of Asia, Africa, and Europe. He knew the climate toward the north and south poles was too harsh to support

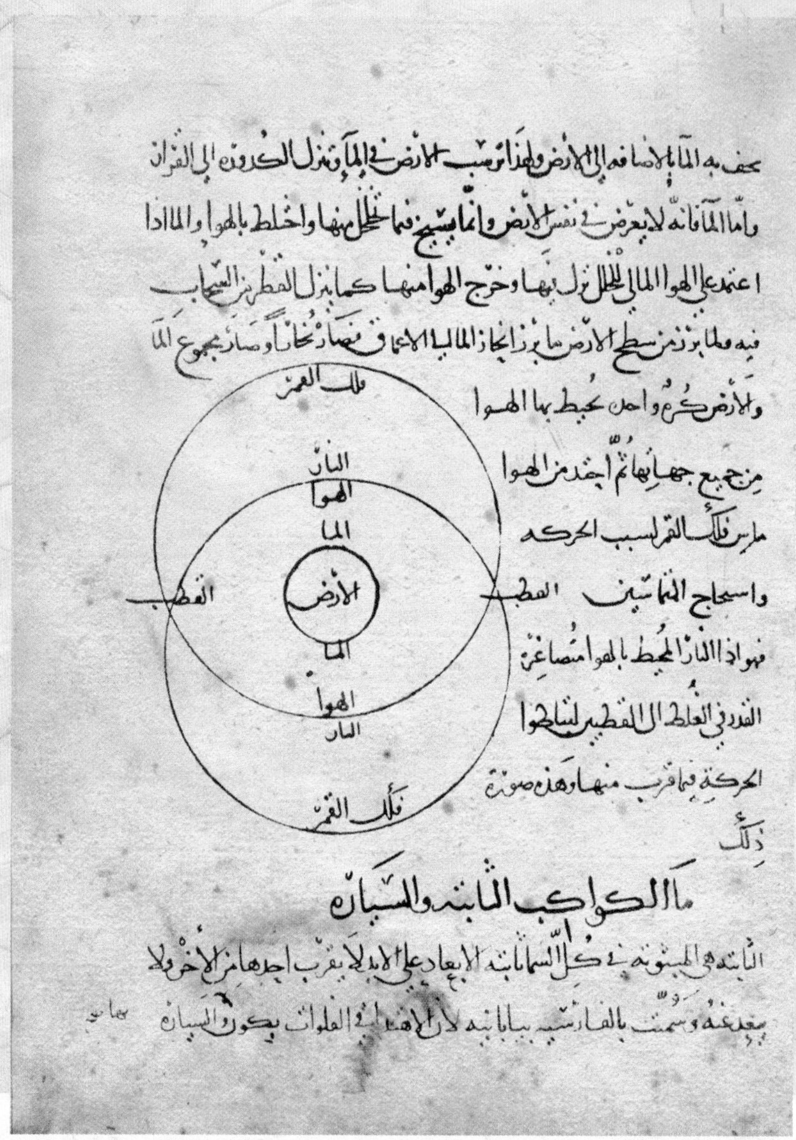

In this text and illustration from al-Biruni's *Instruction in the Elements of the Art of Astrology* (1029), the master astronomer discussed the orbit of the moon and explained that Earth (drawn here as the small circle), which was the center of the moon's orbit, was basically globular in shape and was surrounded by air.

human life and thus hypothesized that roughly one quarter of Earth's surface was habitable by humans. The shores of Asia and Europe, he believed were separated by a vast sea, too dark and dense to navigate and too risky to try.

When it came to his corner of the world, however, no one was more knowledgeable about mapping cities and measuring the distances between them. Combining astronomical readings and mathematic equations, al-Biruni developed methods to pinpoint locations by recording degrees of latitude and longitude. Throughout his life as he traveled across the eastern region of the Middle East and into western India, al-Biruni seized any opportunity to map a new city. He developed similar techniques to measure the heights of mountains, the depths of valleys, and the expanse of the horizon. He documented much of this in his book *The Chronology of Ancient Nations*.

The Natural Sciences and Physics

Al-Biruni's broad interests and endless desire for knowledge are admirable, but what made his work truly remarkable is the level of detail and accuracy he was able to achieve in medieval times working with tools that can only be described as crude by today's standards. His measurements, such as Earth's circumference and the duration of the solar year, were the most accurate of his time and very close to today's measurements. Later in his life, as al-Biruni's interests turned to natural sciences such as medicine and mineralogy, he approached these fields with the same desire for universal truth.

Al-Biruni recorded extensive catalogs of herbs, minerals, metals, and other elements. He went as far as to list these items by name in multiple languages, including Arabic, Greek, Syriac, Persian, Hindi, Latin, and others—illustrating his aptitude for language as well as a desire to make his studies available to a broad range of students. Al-Biruni approached all his work with careful observation, and he recognized the connection between everything he studied regardless of subject matter. In his book *A History of India*, al-Biruni wrote:

> The measure of a thing becomes known by its being compared with another thing which belongs to the same species and is assumed as a unit by general consent. Thereby, the difference between the object and this standard becomes known. By weighing, people determine the amount of gravity of heavy bodies.

Al-Biruni conducted hundreds of experiments to gauge accurate measures of the items he cataloged. His book *Materia Medica (Kitab al-Saidana)* was celebrated for its in-depth studies of minerals and herbs, and *Book of Precious Stones (Kitab al-Jawahir)* is referred to as his era's most complete text on mineralogy. In *Book of Precious Stones*, al-Biruni catalogs each mineral entry by color, odor, hardness, density, and weight. Some weights he calculated out to three decimal points, and many of those differ from modern measurements only at the third decimal place!

Philosophy and Religion

Al-Biruni was a pioneer in the study of comparative religion. Throughout his studies, religion remained at the core of his interest and dedication. He studied Christian, Judaic, Hindu, and Asian religious teachings. His work in religious studies ranks among his most valuable. In the field of philosophy, however, very few of al-Biruni's pure philosophical works exist, so it is difficult to pinpoint his position regarding a philosophical school of thought other than to say that his faith in Islam drove his approach to research and shaped his conclusions.

Al-Biruni wrote in his *Book of Precious Stones* that the possession of intellect makes humans superior to animals and that God, therefore, placed humans as stewards over Earth and other terrestrial life-forms. Al-Biruni viewed hearing and sight as the two most important senses, which humans employ to rise above other creatures. With sight, humans observe the signs of God's divine wisdom in his creations, and through hearing, they receive the word of God and his command. The

This picture of the Qur'anic story of the Annunciation, in which the angel Gabriel announces to Mary that she will give birth to Jesus, is from a 1489 Persian manuscript of al-Biruni's *The Chronology of Ancient Nations*. The text on the page contains al-Biruni's discussion of the Muslim lunar calendar.

heart, al-Biruni wrote, is the true center of intelligence, where sight and hearing meet in an understanding of God's will.

Humans then employ this understanding to reason. Through reason they realize their noble nature and the purpose for which they were created. In this manner, al-Biruni's philosophical position emphasizes al-tawhid, or unity. His philosophy became a guiding principle for cosmological science throughout Muslim history. To have knowledge of things, he believed, is to know from where they originate and, therefore, where they ultimately return. Al-Biruni's works valued the return of humans to God by means of knowledge and purification.

Chapter 3

STRUGGLE AND INSTABILITY

odern scholars debate over the origin of al-Biruni's name. Arabic names are often quite descriptive labels that provide insight into a person's ancestral lineage, occupation, or the region from which they originated. *Biruni* is a Persian word for "outsider." It is typically used to refer to foreigners, but it is unusual as a surname. Although it is possible al-Biruni received his complete name at birth and that "Biruni" was given to his family when they emigrated from Tajikistan, some academics believe al-Biruni received it later in life. One theory suggests that when al-Biruni arrived in Kath from his native suburb to pursue his education, his intelligence immediately set him apart from other outsiders (*birun*), and Kath citizens referred to him as "the outsider." In any event, the name stuck, and al-Biruni spent the first twenty-two years of his life in and around Kath.

The earliest we know al-Biruni was in Kath was in AD 990 when he was seventeen years old. By this time, he was already an accomplished mathematician and astronomer, punctuated by his proficiency with navigational tools such as the sextant, which he likely used to measure the latitude of Kath later that year. Al-Biruni earned his reputation quickly, for it was also in 990 that he was invited to study under Abu Nasr Mansur ibn Iraq's patronage. Abu Nasr Mansur ibn Iraq was just three years older than al-Biruni, but his royal status as prince of the Banu Iraq family afforded him a more formal education under more established teachers than al-Biruni enjoyed before moving to Kath. The older scholar developed a deep respect for al-Biruni and likely viewed him as an academic peer if not a master. He dedicated his first book to al-Biruni in 997. Life at Kath appears to have been generally satisfying for al-Biruni, and he probably would have stayed beyond 995 were he not forced to flee for his life.

FLEEING KHWARIZM

As mentioned previously, al-Biruni was born in a divided region. The region of Khwarizm was split vertically along

Al-Muqanna (also known as Hashim ibn Hakim, "the Veiled One"), a religious leader and commander for Abu Muslim from Khurasan, led a revolt against the Abbasid caliph al-Mahdi. The Abbasids sent troops to al-Muqanna's fortress in Sanam in 779 to capture him. This illustration of the Abbasid siege is found in a 1489 copy of al-Biruni's *The Chronology of Ancient Nations*. Al-Biruni had to flee Khwarizm in 995 because of the political struggles between the Banu Iraq dynasty and the Mamunid dynasty.

the path of the Oxus River, with each side being ruled by an uncompromising dynasty. The western division was under the reign of Abu Ali Mamun bin Muhammad of the Mamunid dynasty, who ruled from the city of Jurjaniyah from 992 to 997. The eastern division, and its capital city at Kath, was part of the Samanid' Empire but ruled by the Iraq dynasty. Power struggles between dynasties were commonplace during the Middle Ages and often escalated into civil war within a region. In 995, Abu Ali Mamun bin Muhammad staged a coup that resulted in the murder of Abu Abd Allah of the Banu Iraq family. Abu Ali Mamun bin Muhammad seized control of Kath and united the rule of the entire Khwarizm region under the Mamunid dynasty.

This double dirham (drachma) silver coin was issued by the Samanid ruler Nuh II, who reigned from 976 to 997. This type of double dirham would have been used in the area where al-Biruni grew up.

Meanwhile, al-Biruni had just finished one of his first important works, a short treatise entitled *Cartography*, on the study of charts and maps. In this book, al-Biruni described calculations for projecting a hemisphere of the globe onto a flat plane. He could then accurately position the locations of the cities for which he had measured and recorded latitudes. Al-Biruni was on his way to inventing what would become the modern map. Unfortunately, the Mamunid conquest halted al-Biruni's work. As a member of the ruling family's court and close associate of Prince Abu Nasr Mansur ibn Iraq, al-Biruni feared his life was in danger. After six years under the

Al-Biruni's world map, or map of the seas, shows south at the top and includes China at the far left, the Sea of Jurjan (Caspian Sea) as the small circle at the left, Iraq near the center, and al-Andalus (Muslim Spain) near the bottom at the right. Some scholars believe that al-Biruni's contribution to cartography is evident in this map because of how he drew the distribution of land and sea. Unlike most mapmakers of his day, al-Biruni depicted the landmass of Africa extending southward instead of east toward China.

patronage of the Banu Iraq dynasty, al-Biruni was still a relatively young man at twenty-two years old. He slipped away from Kath and left behind the entire Khwarizm region. Although he had a brilliant mind, this was likely the first time he found himself truly on his own. The next few years would be quite unsettling for the forlorn scholar.

SURVIVING IN RAYY

Due to his frequent movement during this phase of al-Biruni's life, specific dates are difficult to come by, but we can build a general timeline by tracking his interactions with other scholars. Al-Biruni wandered, unsettled, for a brief period of time following his departure from Khwarizm as he considered a location for his next residence. He was interested in continuing his studies in astronomy, but this would be possible only in a large city that valued academics and had patrons who would support his work. Al-Biruni's options were narrowed down to the three centers of astronomy: Khwarizm, Baghdad, and Rayy. Khwarizm was out of the question for obvious reasons, and Baghdad may have been too far, so al-Biruni settled on Rayy, which was located near present-day Tehran, Iran.

Fakhr al-Dawla ruled the city of Rayy from 976 to 992. Al-Dawla held a great interest in astronomy and had recently

Al-Biruni would probably have used a celestial sphere such as this one to determine a coordinate involving stars or other heavenly bodies. The constellations and stars lie on the globe, concentric with Earth. The sphere is divided by projecting the equator into space, separating the sphere into the north and south celestial hemi-spheres. The directions toward a star or other heavenly body could be measured by creating a coordinate system.

funded the construction of an observatory. Rayy was the kind of city where a renowned astronomer could relocate and find work under the patronage of the reigning court. Unfortunately for al-Biruni, in 996, he was not yet well known outside of Kath. Al-Biruni was unable to find a patron in Rayy and instead lived in poverty. Although he remained confident and continued to study, his poor social standing made him a target of ridicule by established scientists who mocked his theories on the shape of Earth and its rotation.

Al-Khujandi (940–1000) was a respected astronomer at Rayy who regularly conducted experiments at the city's observatory. In 994, he recorded the transit of the sun near the solstices and measured the latitude of Rayy. Al-Biruni found al-Khujandi's results to be inaccurate. In his *The Determination of the Coordinates of Positions for the Correction of Distances Between Cities (Tahdid Nihayat al-Amakin li-Tashih Masafat al-Masakin)*, al-Biruni determined that al-Khujandi's sextant had settled into the ground under its heavy weight, thus throwing off its measurements by twenty-four minutes. Al-Biruni's allegation was correct, and he began to be accepted by other scholars and scientists. His financial status finally improved, but he never gained a place in al-Dawla's court.

In 997, al-Dawla died and was succeeded by Majid al-Dawla Abu Talib Rustum. Al-Biruni solicited the new ruler for a court position and was again denied. Because of its strong reputation, the city simply may have attracted more astronomers than it could support. But the two years al-Biruni spent in Rayy were not in vain. His reputation had spread across the region, and other sultans took notice of him.

THRIVING IN GORGAN

Immediately after the overthrow of Kath, al-Biruni spent time in the refuge of Sultan Nuh ibn Mansur's court at Bukhara. Al-Biruni was probably encouraged to go to Bukhara by his mentor, Abu Nasr Mansur ibn Iraq, who also may have sought protection in his family's court. During his stay at Ibn Mansur's court, al-Biruni met Shams al-Maali bin Qabus, who had recently been removed as ruler of Gorgan. Bin Qabus, too, was a scholar and renowned author, and he became quite impressed with al-Biruni's intellect and passion. In 998, following al-Biruni's latest rejection by the ruling court of Rayy, Bin Qabus regained control over Gorgan. Bin Qabus and al-Biruni must have remained in contact because, upon his reinstatement, the ruler invited al-Biruni to live at his royal residence and study under his patronage. A grateful al-Biruni accepted the offer and returned to full-time academic pursuits.

Al-Biruni resumed his work with a passion. Within two years, he published one of his most important works, *The Chronology of Ancient Nations*, which he dedicated to his patron. Bin Qabus greatly admired his celebrated scholar, and al-Biruni was productive and motivated at Gorgan. Al-Biruni remained under the patronage of Bin Qabus for close to six years, during which time he enjoyed the stability and

The Ark Fortress in Bukhara (which is located in present-day Uzbekistan) was built around 950. Sultan Nuh ibn Mansur's palace was located within the Ark Fortress's walls. Al-Biruni found protection at Ibn Mansur's court, where al-Biruni met Shams al-Maali bin Qabus, the former ruler of Gorgan.

financial security that had eluded him in Rayy. He took full advantage of his good fortune, studying the heavens and recording events such as lunar eclipses, traveling extensively in Persia, mapping the latitudes of additional cities, conducting research, and writing. He completed and dedicated at least one more book to Bin Qabus, his *Treatise on the Skies (Risalah Tajrid al-Sha'at)*.

Once again, al-Biruni found himself in an ideal working situation. He could travel and study without interference, and his fame and fortune grew along with his knowledge and collection of work. There was perhaps one thing that could influence him to leave Gorgan, unfortunately for Bin Qabus, and that thing was evolving in Khwarizm.

Chapter 4

IN THE COURT OF THE MAMUNIDS

Overall, the independent dynasties had a positive impact on the spread of education in Muslim lands. Centers of learning emerged across the Middle East and other areas. Scholars under the patronage of rulers studied full-time and made great strides in scientific advancement, and the culture of knowledge spread to all levels of Muslim society. But to the scholars themselves, their close ties to the ruling courts must have been as frustrating as they were fruitful. Al-Biruni was forced to leave Kath when his patrons were overthrown in a coup; he lived in poverty in Rayy because he could not secure financial support from

This illustration from a fifteenth-century copy of Nezami's five-poem work *Khamseh* depicts a priest bringing a marriage document to Khusrau and is found in the romance poem about Shirin and Khusrau. The Indian artist of the manuscript integrated certain stylistic elements from Persian, Muslim, and Indian paintings. Artists and scholars in Khwarizm thrived in the competitive atmosphere of the Mamunid court, which became much admired as a center of learning.

the court. Once he was thriving away from his homeland, regime change in Khwarizm reversed his exile and courted his return with open arms.

Abu Ali Mamun bin Muhammad was responsible for the overthrow of Kath in 995, which united Khwarizm under his rule and forced al-Biruni to flee the region. The ruler was subsequently executed in 997 and succeeded by his son Abu al-Hasan Ali. Al-Hasan Ali was an effective leader who upheld the strength of the Mamunids and maintained a high regard for education. Under his reign, the united Khwarizm, formerly known for its noble mathematics tradition, emerged as the region's leading center for literature and learning in general. He had a dream to fill his court with the greatest minds of the day, and his court minister Ahmad bin Muhammad al-Suhayli, himself a celebrated scholar, helped make that vision a reality.

Al-Biruni had a competitive nature, which comes across often in his writing. He studied the works of dozens of scholars, from Aristotle to al-Razi, but never accepted their conclusions at face value. He debated his contemporaries with an arrogance that at times bordered on confrontation. In short, al-Biruni believed himself to be the most important scholar of his generation. When al-Hasan Ali recruited him to join his court of prominent scholars, how could al-Biruni say no?

AL-HASAN ALI ASSEMBLES A GROUP OF ACCLAIMED SCHOLARS

In 1004, al-Biruni was thriving under the patronage of Shams al-Maali bin Qabus at Gorgan. Al-Biruni enjoyed a comfortable existence in Bin Qabus's court, but comfort may not have been enough for the ambitious scholar. When al-Hasan Ali came calling, he offered more than just a position at his court; he offered al-Biruni a chance to prove himself the leader in his field. Khwarizm was known for mathematics and astronomy and had risen in prestige since al-Biruni left. A return would be a step up from Gorgan in terms of his reputation as an astronomer. Similarly, al-Hasan Ali had assembled a superior group of academics, and al-Biruni recognized the honor of being part of such a select team. He agreed to leave Gorgan and join al-Hasan Ali's court.

Al-Hasan Ali placed a high value on knowledge and backed up this ideal with generous funding of his library and court. It was this liberal funding that led to his extraordinary collection of scientists and philosophers. As promised, al-Hasan Ali's court boasted the finest minds in the region. Abu al-Khayr Khummar (967–1049) excelled in the area of medicine, Ibn Sina and Abu Sahl Masihi (971–1011) were the leading scholars on Greek philosophy and science, al-Biruni's former mentor Abu Nasr Mansur ibn Iraq was the resident mathematics

Ibn Sina (Avicenna, circa 992–1037), a leading scholar in Aristotelian philosophy and medicine, was among the group of philosophers and scientists who studied and wrote books at al-Hasan Ali's court in Khwarizm. Al-Biruni and Ibn Sina worked together on several scientific projects for their patron.

expert, and al-Biruni himself rounded out the group with his primary focus on astronomy.

Because the court employed specialists in various fields, each scholar had the freedom to focus on his particular area

Al-Biruni Vs. Aristotle: Taking on the Peripatetics

Peripatetics are followers of Aristotle who often teach his works and methods. Al-Biruni had a significant problem with Peripatetics because their philosophy is based on blindly accepting and furthering Aristotle's methodology often to the point of believing Aristotle to be infallible. In his work, al-Biruni had the capacity to study objectively and separate fact from faith. When he researched the theories of Aristotle, al-Biruni put Aristotle's methods into practice and determined accuracy through experimentation and reason, sometimes proving the conclusion correct while disproving the method. But upon presenting his findings, debate would inevitably ensue with Peripatetics, who were resistant to new ideas. In other cases, al-Biruni proved Aristotle's conclusions to be flat-out wrong, yet the Peripatetic reaction would be the same. For example, Aristotle believed vision was the product of rays emanating from one's eyes and focusing on an object; al-Biruni challenged this theory and wrote that vision is actually the result of light rays bouncing off an object toward one's eyes. Another correction involved the location of the stars; al-Biruni rejected Aristotle's assertion that the stars were positioned inside the orbital rings of the planets and instead determined that they are at the farthest reaches of the galaxy. Al-Biruni confidently championed his conclusions against Peripatetic doctrines, which he argued were based too heavily on rationalization and not enough on scientific experimentation. According to al-Biruni, scientific experimentation leads to factual information and reinforces the teachings of Islam.

of expertise. Each also had the benefit of working closely with other gifted scholars, with whom they would share ideas and collaborate to solve problems. Al-Biruni and Abu Nasr Mansur ibn Iraq, for example, renewed their rewarding working relationship. Al-Biruni had an observatory erected in Jurjaniyah where he observed solar median transits and regularly conducted experiments. The outstanding team of scholars generated a wealth of texts and treatises for their patron, and their association was unique in history.

Competition, too, motivated al-Hasan Ali's court. These men were confident in their abilities and eager to prove their intelligence to one another, which facilitated healthy debate and rivalry as the scholars raced to uncover new truths. Out of this rivalry, Ibn Sina and al-Biruni emerged as the clear leaders and earned the utmost respect of their colleagues. The two managed to find a way to work together, but it is likely that their growing bases of followers may have clashed as the students debated the methods of their mentors.

THE RISE AND FALL OF AL-ABBAS

Khwarizm's team of scholars was still intact in 1009 when al-Hasan Ali died and his brother Abu al-Abbas assumed power. Al-Abbas pledged to continue al-Hasan Ali's policies, but he did not possess the effective leadership skills of his brother; thus, the Mamunid dynasty's days were numbered. Al-Abbas

لَئِنْ كَانَ فَقَالَ إِنَّا لِلّٰهِ وَأُفَوِّضُ أَمْرِي إِلَى اللّٰهِ وَلَا حَوْلَ وَلَا قُوَّةَ إِلَّا بِاللّٰهِ

لِمَنْ يَقِ صَافٍ وَلَا مُصَافٍ وَلَا مُعِينٍ وَلَا مُعِينٍ

وَفِي الْمَبَادِي بَدْءُ النِّيادِي فَلَا أَمِينٍ وَلَا ثَمِينٍ

ثُمَّ قَالَ لَهَا مِنِّي النَّفِيسُ وَعَدَّهَا وَأَجْمَعَي الرِّقَاعَ وَعَدَّهَا فَقَالَتْ لَقَدْ عَدَدْتُهَا لَمَّا

اسْتَعَدْتُهَا فُوحَدِّثَتْ بِيَدِ الضِّبَاعِ فَقَالَتْ أَجْدِبُ الرِّقَاعَ فَقَالَ يُعْنَالُكِ الْكَلَامُ الْجَمُّ

was unable to maintain cordial relations with al-Suhayli, and as a result, in 1013, the minister of the court left for Baghdad. Al-Suhayli had played a key role in assembling the team of academics. In his absence, al-Biruni assumed advisory responsibilities and rose in political influence; in fact, he may have been on track to become court minister. But Ibn Sina and Abu Sahl Masihi reacted to al-Suhayli's departure differently; they decided to leave as well.

Meanwhile the Ghaznavid dynasty, which ruled from 962 to 1186, had acquired control of nearby Khurasan. While al-Hasan Ali was still alive, he cemented an alliance with the Ghaznavids by marrying Kah-Kalji, the sister of Ghaznavid leader Mahmud. Mahmud intimidated al-Abbas and so upon al-Hasan Ali's death, al-Abbas married his brother's widow to maintain the alliance. Recognizing al-Abbas's weakness, Mahmud insisted al-Abbas declare loyalty to him by enforcing religious leaders to acknowledge Mahmud's name as ruler during the Khutbah, the Friday sermon from the pulpit that preceded public prayer at each mosque. In his paranoia, al-Abbas instead

A Persian literary text from the thirteenth century illustrates Abu Zayd preaching from the pulpit in a mosque. The text is based on the *Maqamat* (Assemblies), a book by the Arab writer al-Hariri (circa 1054–1122) of Basra. Mahmud demanded that al-Abbbas declare loyalty to him during the Khutbah, the Friday sermon from the pulpit.

Sultan Mahmud of Ghaznah is pictured here seated on his throne. This illustration is from a fifteenth-century Persian manuscript of the epic poem *Shahnameh* (The Book of Kings), written by the Persian poet Ferdowsi around 1000. Mahmud seized control of Khwarizm in 1017 and had al-Biruni and two other scholars taken to his court at Ghaznah.

attempted to forge a new alliance with the Turkish khan Ilak of Kashgar. Al-Biruni advised al-Abbas to pacify both sides, but after a botched negotiation, al-Abbas felt his only choice was to concede to Mahmud's demand. The Khutbah was recited in Mahmud's name in all cities except Jurjaniy and Khwarizm. This compromise satisfied Mahmud but incited anger in al-Abbas's own subjects, who viewed their leader as a coward. In 1017, insubordinate soldiers led by Alaptgin Bukhari attacked and killed al-Abbas.

Although he was somewhat responsible for the death of al-Abbas, the ambitious Mahmud saw the situation as an opportunity to take control of Khwarizm. Later that year, he launched a successful conquest in the name of avenging his brother-in-law's death. Had Mahmud known of al-Biruni's advice to al-Abbas to continue his alliance with the Turks, Mahmud likely would have had al-Biruni executed. Instead, Mahmud brought the three remaining scholars, al-Biruni, Abu Nasr Mansur ibn Iraq, and al-Khayr Khummar, to his court at Ghaznah, which is located in present-day Afghanistan. Al-Biruni later noted the details of the fall of Abu al-Abbas and the transfer of power to Mahmud in his book *The Revolution of Khwarizm (Masamir-i-Khwaritzm)*, which he was careful not to write until after Mahmud's death in 1030.

Chapter 5

IN THE COURT OF
THE GHAZNAVIDS

A l-Biruni had no choice but to join Mahmud's court. He and 5,000 others were taken as prisoners of war from Khwarizm and held at Mahmud's capital city of Ghaznah. Although Islamic religion condemns slavery, it was a fairly common practice for warring dynasties to coerce talent to join their courts. These "slaves" had the potential to rise in prominence in the court and actually gain status typically reserved for the aristocracy. Mahmud was familiar with the reputations of al-Biruni and his fellow scholars at al-Abbas's court prior to the conquest. In fact, he had made previous attempts to recruit them to his

Mahmud Ghaznavi *(left)* seized the fortress of Asi in India. Over the course of his reign (998–1030), Mahmud invaded India seventeen times, from 1001 to 1026. A great warrior, a champion of Islam, and a renowned patron of the arts, Mahmud extended the Ghaznavid rule into central Asia and helped to further the exchange of trade and scholarship between Muslim lands and India. Among the scholars whom Mahmud encouraged to study at Ghaznah were al-Biruni and the Persian poet Ferdowsi.

court. Al-Biruni was embraced as a valuable addition to the kingdom of Ghaznah and encouraged to continue his studies under Mahmud's patronage. Over the course of the next two years, we have no record of al-Biruni traveling outside Ghaznah, which may be an indication of his detention. In his book *The Revolution of Khwarizm*, al-Biruni humbly wrote about his patron, "Mahmud did not grudge me any good

Indian officials are presented to Mahmud (far right) in this illustration from the *Compendium of Chronicles*, a multivolume history and geography about the Mongols and Eurasian peoples written by Rashid al-Din (1247–1318). Al-Biruni learned Sanskrit and Indian dialects from the Hindus who lived in Ghaznah, until he was allowed to accompany Mahmud on military expeditions into northern India, including Kashmir, a leading center of learning. Al-Biruni sought to study Indian astronomy and geography with scholars there.

things of life; he made me rich and bypassed my harsh demands." Indeed, Mahmud provided a comfortable existence for his scholars, but al-Biruni never had the type of respectful relationship with Mahmud that he enjoyed with other patrons.

The conquest of Khwarizm was just one of many victories Mahmud orchestrated as a military leader. He expanded his realm into a large empire that united central Asia from Iran to western India. As a result, although al-Biruni was stuck in Ghaznah between 1018 and 1020, he continued to gain exposure to new knowledge and ideas, particularly from members of the court who traveled with Mahmud on his excursions to the eastern region of the Punjab and Kashmir. It was likely during this period that al-Biruni developed his fascination with the Hindu religion and Indian culture. Scholars suggest that he took advantage of his time in Ghaznah to become expert in Sanskrit—the written language of India—and Indian dialects, which would become instrumental in his future studies. Al-Biruni also had access to an observatory at Ghaznah where he continued to conduct his astronomy experiments and geographical studies. These include observations of solar and lunar eclipses, recorded between April and September 1019.

A PROLIFIC PERIOD OF STUDY AND TRAVEL

The circumstances that brought al-Biruni to Mahmud's court were neither of his choosing nor under his control. Once again, he saw his studies interrupted by politics and his life uprooted as he was transferred to a new situation. But al-Biruni found inspiration in Ghaznah. In Khwarizm, al-Biruni had the opportunity to study in one of the world's leading centers for astronomy and other scientific studies. At Ghaznah, he had the unique opportunity to *create* a center of excellence in these fields through his reputation, research, and writing. As he studied the scientific theories of India, al-Biruni recognized an untapped pool of knowledge, which he exploited as a vehicle for his breakthrough work. Al-Biruni insisted upon studying Indian books in their original Sanskrit because he demanded nothing less than the absolute truth and feared human error in translated versions. In a famous episode that exemplifies his passion, al-Biruni conducted an ultimately successful forty-year search for the Indian work *Book of India (Safar al-Israr)* by Mani, the founder of the Manichaeism religion.

When he was free to travel, al-Biruni accompanied Mahmud on at least one of his conquests into India and made several other independent treks into the subcontinent with the sultan's permission. These expeditions took place between 1020 and 1029 and focused on the northwest portion of the country. During his travels to India, al-Biruni studied the country's culture, religion, environment, literature, and scientific theory firsthand. Most of this research is well documented in his book *A History of India (Tarikh al-Hind)*. He measured the latitudes of the Indian cities through which he traveled, including major centers such as Kashmir, Varanasi, and Multan—a pilgrimage center of Hinduism—and recorded directions and distances between

This fourteenth-century Egyptian manuscript depicts travelers on their way to India. Because of Mahmud's conquests in northwestern India, members of the army and court came back to Ghaznah with stories about and treasures from the lands and people they encountered during their exploits. Al-Biruni became interested in studying Indian culture and learned to read and write Sanskrit.

them. Along the way, al-Biruni developed relationships with local teachers and gained access to the books of Hindu scholar Balabhadra. Upon returning to Ghaznah, he remained in contact with some of these teachers and continued his studies through correspondence with them.

والمعتدله هي بُعده فيه عن الذروه المرتبه وفضل ما بينهما

هو تعديل لخاصه الاول ﴿ ما الطول الاوسط والمعدل

اما الاوسط فمقدار التي يحيط بها الخارجان من مركز

الفلك المعَدل للمسير الى اوجه والى مركز التدوير واما المعدل

فمقدار الزاويه التي يحيط بها الخطان الخارجان من مركز

العالم الى اوج المعَدل للمسير والى مركز التدويره وفضل ما

بينهما هو تعديل الطول وهو مقدار الزاويه الحادثه

من الخطوط المذكوره عند مركز التدوير وربما سمي الطول مركزًا

﴿ ما تعديل الحصه الثانيه في مقدار الزاويه التي يحيط بها الخطان

الخارجان من مركز العالم الى كل واحد من مركز التدوير وجرم الكوكب

﴿ ما تقوم الكوكب هي النقطه من الفلك الممثل التي ينتهي اليها

الخط الخارج من مركز العالم الى جرم الكوكب وذلك موضعه الذي يرى

فيه من فلك البروج وهذه صوره ذكر

توضيح كيف افلاك القمر

له فلك ممثل

وفلك مايل عنه

وذلك اوج لحمل

فلك تدويره

الذي يدور

جر مـــه

علــيـــه

But al-Biruni's studies in Ghaznah were not limited to India. By 1029, he had completed several written works, including his *Book of Coordinates*; two treatises on mathematics; and *Instruction in the Elements of the Art of Astrology (Kitab al-Tafhim)*, a simple book covering the elements of astronomy and dedicated to Lady Rayhanah of the Khwarizm court. In addition, he recorded latitudes of several cities located in present-day Afghanistan and conducted his era's most accurate measurement of Earth's circumference from a mountaintop in Nandana utilizing a complex formula of his own creation, based on advanced trigonometry.

PATRONAGE AND RESPECT UNDER MASUD

Al-Biruni reluctantly served in Mahmud's court for thirteen years, but he had no regrets because the scope of his studies expanded under Mahmud's patronage in ways he could not have predicted. In 1030, Mahmud passed away and his youngest son, Muhammad, succeeded him to the Ghaznavid

Al-Biruni's book *Instruction in the Elements of the Art of Astrology* (1029) included this page about the orbit or path of a celestial body. Besides his book on India and *Book of Coordinates*, al-Biruni completed this book on astronomy while at Ghaznah.

throne. Shortly thereafter, in 1031, Muhammad's own brother Masud wrested control of the empire for himself, locking his sibling in a Taginabad prison. During this brief period of turmoil and uncertainty, al-Biruni feared that he would be released from the court and forced to seek patronage elsewhere. Although it was not his decision to come to Ghaznah in the first place, al-Biruni was now fifty-eight years old and it *was* his choice to stay. Al-Biruni was concerned about losing the work he had amassed over the past decade and wary of being on his own in his advancing age. As it turned out, al-Biruni had nothing to fear. Masud, himself an avid astronomer, had great respect for al-Biruni and encouraged him to continue his work without pause.

Al-Biruni developed with Masud a relationship based upon mutual admiration that he had never had with Mahmud. The sultan befriended al-Biruni and provided the now famed scholar with wealth beyond his imagination. One legendary account relates that, when al-Biruni included his patron's name in the title of his greatest work on astronomy, *Astronomy and Trigonometry (Al-Qanun al-Mas'udi)*, Masud rewarded the scholar with an elephant-load of silver. Al-Biruni was overwhelmed but graciously rejected the generous gift. Al-Biruni repeatedly acknowledged his gratitude for the support of Masud and compared it to his situation under Bin Qabus while working in Gorgan. Bin Qabus enabled al-Biruni to have direct participation in state affairs,

The Turkish astronomer Takiuddin and others study the skies and work in the observatory at Galata, Istanbul, in 1577. This illustration is from *Shahnameh* (Book of the Kings) which was written for Sultan Murad III. It shows the astronomers using various instruments such as an astrolabe *(right)*; an alidade that is connected to a quadrant *(left)*; and a diopter *(top left)*, which is a measuring tool with viewing apertures. Al-Biruni would have used many instruments similar to these while working at observatories.

while Masud provided an environment that allowed him to devote his time and energy completely to the pursuit of knowledge. Both privileges were reserved only for the most respected members of the court.

Al-Biruni wrote other books for Masud as a way to educate the sultan on topics in which he showed interest. One such example is *The Book of Night and Day (Kitab layl wa al-Nahar)*, another work on astronomy. Masud posed questions regarding the varying duration of day and night at different parts of the world, particularly at the poles, where he heard the sun never set. Al-Biruni's answers came in the form of this brief treatise, which was dedicated to his patron and written at a basic level that was easy for Masud to understand.

THE FINAL DAYS OF AL-BIRUNI'S LIFE

Al-Biruni was struck with more uncertainty in 1039 when Masud was defeated in battle by the Seljuqs, who took over control of Khurasan. Upon Masud's retreat, his brother Muhammad was freed from prison and reemerged to orchestrate a revolt that culminated in Masud's death. Masud's son Mawdud came to his father's defense, executed Muhammad and his son Ahmad, and eventually gained the throne, ruling until 1049. Although these events must have caused more anxiety for al-Biruni, things did not change much under Mawdud's rule. Mawdud was known for his justice and good character. Al-Biruni continued with his studies under Mawdud's patronage, living in comfort and respect in his court. During this time, he completed his works on mineralogy: *Book of Precious Stones*, *Book of Rules (Kitab al-Dastur)*, and others dedicated to his last patron.

Al-Biruni died in Ghaznah in 1048. He lived the final years of his life under the fear that he would not complete all the work he set out to accomplish, and indeed, he continued studying until his last breath. Al-Biruni's last complete book was *Materia Medica*, which he wrote with great difficulty as his eyesight and mental capacity were fading—repetition and omission of facts in this book are uncharacteristic of his typical work. A final act illustrates al-Biruni's truly unrivaled passion for knowledge. Upon his deathbed, al-Biruni is said to have asked Faqih Abu al-Hasan, an expert on Islamic law, to teach him something. Al-Hasan complied and described the account of Jadat al-Fasidah, a legal case involving corruption. Al-Biruni memorized the account and repeated it back. Shortly thereafter, the extraordinary Muslim scholar passed away.

Chapter 6

A MASTER OF ASTRONOMY

Because the unknowns of the universe are so often associated with spiritual entities, the science of astronomy has always been controversial—and so it was in al-Biruni's lifetime. Some Muslims viewed the study of the heavens as heresy because much of the existing writing on the subject was the product of Aristotle and the Greek philosophers. The Greek philosophers were considered heathens for their lack of knowledge of God and the practice of projecting their gods upon the sky in the form of stellar constellations. Indeed, at times al-Biruni had to practice caution when conducting his research, or else risk imprisonment.

There were, of course, several practical uses of astronomy, such as navigation and time measurement. Al-Biruni was instrumental in perfecting these applications, which even the most conservative Muslims had to appreciate. In the end, al-Biruni conducted all his studies in the name of Islam and in constant pursuit of truth and a deeper connection with the Creator.

Al-Biruni likely viewed astronomy as the pinnacle of science, bringing together disciplines such as mathematics, physics, natural science, and geography to explain the universal harmony of nature. He believed this work to be the highest order of Islamic faith and pointed out several religious arguments for the study of astronomy. He even referenced passages from the Qur'an, such as, "God asks people to contemplate on the marvels of the earth and heavens." Al-Biruni wrote his book *Treatise on the Direction of Prayer (Risalah fi al-ab ath al-Tashih al-Qiblah)* to demonstrate how astronomy can be used to help Muslims locate the city of Mecca. This information was instrumental to constructing mosques, which are built to face the holy city, and vital in saying the daily prayers (Salat). Muslims recite the Kiblah prayers five times per day in the direction of Mecca. More controversial than astronomy was the subject of astrology, which al-Biruni also studied and in which he was likewise considered an expert. Astrology focuses on the constellations of stars that make up the signs of the zodiac and

Pictured here is a page from a 1505 book for pilgrims showing the Kaaba at Mecca. Al-Biruni explained how astronomy could be used to help Muslims locate the city of Mecca in his *Treatise on the Direction of Prayer*. Builders referred to this information to orient the position of mosques. Mosques are constructed to face Mecca because Muslims turn toward that direction to recite prayers.

the rhythm of their movement, which some people believe influences events on Earth. Though not typically considered a science today, astrology was very closely tied to astronomy during the medieval period and held scientific, if not psychic, value to al-Biruni.

AL-BIRUNI'S THEORY OF THE UNIVERSE

In astronomy, as in the other sciences he studied, al-Biruni began his research by consuming as much relevant information as possible in order to take full advantage of the work conducted by those scientists and scholars who came before him. As a result, al-Biruni's fundamental view of the universe was rooted in the conventional thinking of his day, which originated in ancient Grecian ideas. Beyond that initial research stage, however, he would conduct his own exhaustive experiments to prove or disprove existing theories and determine a baseline truth in the field. Finally, driven by his commitment to Islam and the desire to further the collective human knowledge, he developed and tested new theories in an attempt to answer unexplained phenomena and increase humanity's understanding of the universe.

Al-Biruni accepted the geocentric theory of the universe, which is the belief that Earth is at the center of a spherical galaxy. He explained that although Earth rotates on its axis, it remains relatively still while the other celestial bodies of the universe revolve around it. Surrounding Earth were eight rings that wrapped around each other like the layers of an onion. These rings were the tracks on which celestial bodies orbited Earth. In expanding order from closest to farthest from Earth, al-Biruni identified the following bodies: the Moon, Mercury, Venus, the Sun, Mars, Jupiter, and Saturn. Al-Biruni believed the rings had width, which allowed the bodies to travel in a looping motion within their tracks as they orbited Earth. This explained distance fluctuations between these bodies and Earth. Beyond the seven orbital rings was an eighth ring, a relatively static band of stars, including the twelve constellations of the zodiac. Al-Biruni alleged that the planets generated their own light just as the Sun and stars do. Consequently, he placed the Sun's orbit beyond the orbits of Mercury and Venus because their brilliance does not diminish as they move farther away from Earth, which would be the case if they existed beyond the brightness of the Sun.

Al-Biruni's geocentric theory of the universe was logical and served him well in his astronomical measurements and experiments, but it was not completely accurate because it was the product of research using crude tools. The idea of a heliocentric universe, wherein planets revolve around the Sun, existed in al-Biruni's day but could not yet be confirmed as fact. Al-Biruni was very familiar with the theory and had even taken measurements with Abu Said al-Sijzi's heliocentric-based astrolabe, an ancient tool used to track celestial bodies.

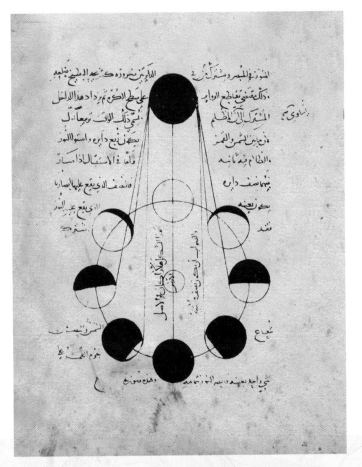

Al-Biruni included a discussion of the moon and its brightness due to the sun in his book *Instruction in the Elements of the Art of Astrology*. He wrote *Key of Astronomy* to explain and defend his geocentric theory of the universe.

He concluded that the conflicting theories did not affect the movement of the heavens relative to time and direction and refused to support an unproven new theory. Al-Biruni wrote *Key of Astronomy (Miftah 'ilm al-Hai'ah)* to explain

Al-Biruni Vs. Aristotle: The Origin of the Universe

In his writings on the origin of the universe, Aristotle hypothesized the universe was eternal, with neither a beginning nor an end. Al-Biruni rejected the celebrated Greek philosopher's theory. He believed that God created the universe, thus establishing its beginning. He further surmised that the universe would have an end, which, too, would be determined and controlled by the Creator. Based on the existence of shells and fossils he discovered in regions that once housed seas and later evolved into dry ground areas, in his geographic work *Book of Coordinates*, al-Biruni wrote that Earth is constantly evolving geologically and things have not always been as they appear. This evolution, he believed, proved Earth to be a living entity. Al-Biruni's theory was directly in concert with Islam, which teaches that even the mightiest of earthly powers and the greatest human achievements will crumble in the face of God. Nothing is truly eternal, neither living objects nor inanimate ones, such as mountains and rocks. He further believed Earth had an age, though its origin was too distant to measure. In this respect, al-Biruni's theory was in sync with the current scientific majority.

his position on the subject. Respected scholars argued on opposite sides of the debate—Ibn Sina embraced the heliocentric theory, while Abu Nasr Mansur ibn Iraq supported the geocentric side. Also up for debate during al-Biruni's time was the composition of the Sun. Al-Biruni theorized the Sun to be a fiery body, which is in line with modern scientists. He based his opinion on studies of total solar eclipses, during which he observed solar flares that he correctly defined as flames erupting and rising up into the atmosphere.

MEASUREMENTS AND OTHER WORKS

Astronomy is truly an all-encompassing science, combining elements of mathematics, geography, and other disciplines, so it should come as no surprise that al-Biruni's achievements in astronomy cover a broad spectrum. From time measurement to mapmaking, al-Biruni constantly approached this vast field of science from a theoretical standpoint, applied abstract concepts to draw conclusions, and finally produced results that were relevant to daily Muslim life. His work consistently achieved its objectives of connecting all things, defining truths in harmony with the teachings of Islam, and reinforcing the relationship between God and humankind.

Al-Biruni had great respect for al-Sijzi and the accuracy of his heliocentric astrolabe, but in typical fashion, he felt it necessary to invent his own instrument. Al-Biruni developed his own astrolabe, which he named al-Ustawani. In addition to celestial bodies and their movement, al-Biruni's astrolabe could measure inaccessible earthly locations such as the heights of mountains and depths of wells. So important to his work was the astrolabe that al-Biruni wrote several treatises

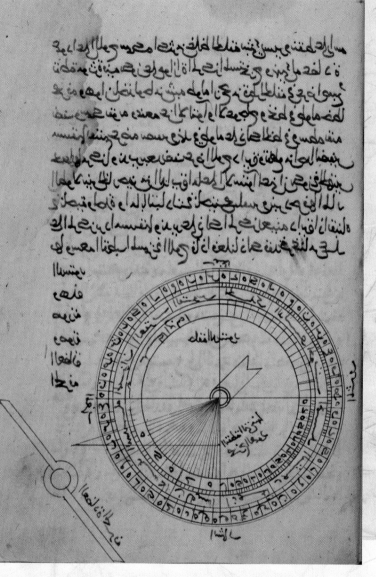

This illustration is from al-Biruni's treatise on the construction of the astrolabe. Al-Biruni made his own astrolabe, which he called al-Ustawani. His astrolabe helped him to measure the heights of mountains, among other land features.

on its function including *Procedures Necessary for Building an Astrolabe (Kitab fi Isti'ab Al-Wujuh Al-Mum Kina fi San'at Al-Asturlab)*, which describes its use in his method for measuring the circumference of Earth. Al-Biruni measured Earth's circumference to be 24,778.24 miles (39,964.9 kilometers). This was the most accurate calculation of Earth's circumference during the Middle Ages and less than 200 miles (322 km) off the current mark. But he assumed Earth to be a perfect sphere, which it is not. Today, we know that Earth bows out at the equator; however, if the modern-day measurement of its circumference were adjusted to assume a perfect sphere, it would be almost identical to al-Biruni's calculation. Al-Biruni also measured the distances of all the orbiting bodies (at their closest and farthest points); the full diameter of the galaxy, from one end of the zodiac to the other; and countless other spans.

Even though his geocentric assumption was incorrect, al-Biruni's calculations of the duration of a solar year were the most accurate of his era. Al-Biruni studied several existing calculations before conducting his own experiments, and his final conclusion was 365 days, 5 hours, and 49 minutes. This figure differs from current calculations by less than 15 minutes! Similarly, al-Biruni calculated the duration of the lunar month to the most accurate measurement of the day, and he explained in great detail the effects the phases of the Moon have on the ocean tides. With regard to the stars, al-Biruni recognized the limitations of his tools and did not attempt to verify counts or measurements that he knew would be inaccurate.

Al-Biruni was an expert in measuring latitudes, and he recorded the latitudes of more than 600 locations during his life. Finding longitudes was more difficult, but he devised three methods for determining this measurement as well. With these figures known, al-Biruni would create models of the known hemisphere and place indicators on it showing the positions of cities by latitude and longitude coordinates. He could then apply his expertise in spherical trigonometry to accurately convert the hemisphere onto a flat plane. These two functions combined produced the first accurate maps, and in his inventive work *The Determination of the Coordinates of Positions for the Correction of Distances Between Cities (Tahdid Nihayat al-Amakin li-Tashih Masafat al-Masakin)*, al-Biruni placed the fixed boundaries of several countries and cities on map pages. Al-Biruni is often referred to as the father of geodesy for his innovative achievements in this field.

THE STUDY OF ASTROLOGY AS SCIENCE

In al-Biruni's day, astrology went hand in hand with astronomy, and he was acclaimed as the leading mind in both fields. In fact, half of al-Biruni's book *Instruction in the Elements in the Art of Astrology (Kitab al-Tafhim li Awa'il Sina'at al-Tanjim)* focuses on astrology. Al-Biruni collected

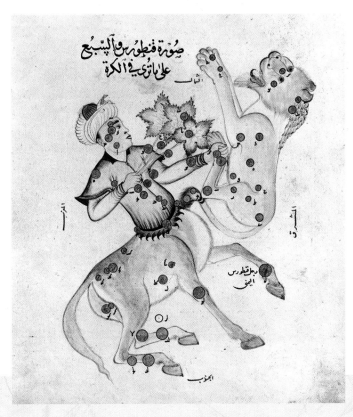

This is a fifteenth-century illustration from *Treatise on the Fixed Stars* by the Persian astronomer Abd al-Rahman al-Sufi (903–986) that shows the constellations of Centaurus and Leo. Al-Sufi's book included information on forty-eight constellations, such as those found in the star charts that had been compiled by the Alexandrian astronomer Ptolemy in the second century. There were also two perspectives of each constellation given, one as it appeared to a viewer on Earth and the other as it would appear on the celestial sphere as seen from space. Al-Biruni studied preceding astronomical texts such as that by al-Sufi, who was born in Rayy.

learning on astrology from existing Greek, Iranian, and Indian understanding and processed it through his own knowledge of mathematics and astronomy to further develop it as a science. Today, we associate astrology with horoscopes and fortune-telling. These elements were present in al-Biruni's time as well, but he did not subscribe to them. Instead, in his *Instruction in the Elements in the Art of Astrology*, al-Biruni wrote, "The system of predictions in astrology rests on totally absurd principles, weak deductions, contradictory guesses, and mere assumptions, opposed to certainties."

Al-Biruni used astrology as a numerology tool to categorize elements and other earthly cycles and functions. He valued astrological symbols as identifiers but did not view astrology as an exact science. Nor did he look to it for answers to questions. The signs of the zodiac are grouped into four triads. Each triad represents one of the four natural elements (heat, cold, moisture, and dryness); each member of the triad represents a fundamental tendency of the spirit (descending movement, horizontal, and ascent); and each sign represents a duality principle (male/female, active/passive, fertile/barren, etc.). It follows that the twelve signs comprise all the elements of the universe, so when al-Biruni studied the human body as a microcosm, he was able to use the signs to pinpoint any area of human anatomy. Astrology then leads to early forms of medicine because the signs can also be used to isolate ailments and identify corresponding cures, as the same universal elements exist in medicinal plants and herbs. In this way, astrology fits nicely into al-Biruni's philosophy of divine unity in all God's creations.

Chapter 7

AL-BIRUNI'S KEY WRITINGS

A l-Biruni was a man of books at a time when books were literally worth their weight in gold. In fact, a Muslim scholar named Hunayn ibn Ishaq (808–873) reportedly received an amount of gold equal to the weight of each book he translated from Greek into Arabic. Understanding his limitless passion for knowledge, it almost goes without saying that al-Biruni read every relevant book he could get his hands on. He must have taken great pride in his ability to write books of his own, which in turn influenced so many of his peers and followers. Indeed, his *Instruction in the Elements in the Art of Astrology* was a major source for works by Yaqut ibn Abdallah al-Hamawi and Mazhar al-Din Muhammad al-Lara, who lived and worked 200 and 500 years respectively after al-Biruni's death.

Al-Biruni referred to the pen as the everlasting monument of history. In *A History of India*, al-Biruni wrote, "No one will deny that in questions of historic authenticity, hearsay does not equal eye-witness." So when learning new information from other people, he always made a point to put it into writing. Al-Biruni wrote clearly and arranged his data logically. In an attempt to keep his reader's interest, he at times veers off subject to talk about a related topic before returning to the original subject. But he likens these subjects to gardens, saying that leaving one garden to visit another reignites the reader's attention. In his writing, al-Biruni explains everything and never refers to a new subject without having introduced it earlier. A great champion of the Arabic language, he called it the best communication tool of his day.

Al-Biruni wrote numerous important books that are often referred to as the pinnacle sources of his era in their particular fields of study. In an all too brief attempt to illustrate the breadth and depth of his work, this chapter focuses on two books that cover very broad topics and were written at very different stages in al-Biruni's life.

THE CHRONOLOGY OF ANCIENT NATIONS

Al-Biruni's first passion in his pursuit of knowledge was astronomy. Chronology, the study of the sequence of events over time, is inherently related to astronomy because astronomy is the tool used to measure time. Likewise, chronology is fundamental to astronomy, as dates and times must be defined in order to record individual events marked by the movement of celestial bodies. Al-Biruni in his astronomy work was already dedicated to learning everything he could about calendars and chronology. He endeavored to understand differences in time measurement by various cultures as well as how the duration of daylight changes in various parts of the world, such as at the poles of Earth. Until he had this depth of knowledge, al-Biruni felt his findings could not be applied as universal truths.

Al-Biruni wrote his masterpiece *Kitab al-Athar al-Baqiyah ani-l-qurun al-Khaliya* in 1000 when he was only twenty-seven years old. This book, which we refer to in English as *The Chronology of Ancient Nations*, is recognized as the best source of Middle Eastern history in medieval times. Al-Biruni completed the book during his time in Gorgan studying under the patronage of Shams al-Maali bin Qabus. He gratefully dedicated *The Chronology* to his patron in return for al-Biruni's favorable position in Bin Qabus's court, which afforded al-Biruni the time to research and write this celebrated volume.

As stated in the preface to *The Chronology*, al-Biruni was inspired to write the book because "it throws light on the residuary customs of past nations through understanding information, news, and traditions." Al-Biruni researched all existing methods of time measurement and attempted to develop a new, more accurate methodology, employing sunlight, shadows, and complex geometry—skills developed through his mathematics and astronomy studies. Using this method, he defined universal time durations for day and night, lunar months, and solar years. He presented a detailed account of various calendars in use and then converted the differing dates to his universal timeline. Once completed, he plotted all well-known important historical events on the timeline to illustrate their occurrences in relation to one another, making the work the first comprehensive history, from the birth of Adam to the origin of Islam to AD 1000.

Muslim scholars studied various cultures and religions prior to al-Biruni's *Chronology*, but only on parallel timelines. Often they could not understand the time relationship between events that occurred in different regions nor could

This is the frontispiece of al-Biruni's *The Chronology of Ancient Nations*, from a 1489 edition. Considered al-Biruni's masterpiece, *The Chronology* (1000) was the standard reference on the history of Muslim territories for centuries.

كتاب الآثار الباقية عن القرون الخالية

تأليف الحكيم العالم البارع الأكمل الأفضل ناصر
الدين مهندس الآفاق نادرة الفلك أعجوبة العالم محمد بن احمد
المكنى أبي الريحان البيروني الخوارزمي رحمه الله

they accurately track a sequence of events across two or more cultures because each had its own calendar system. *The Chronology* opened up the opportunity for future scholars to study history across all regions and nations.

A HISTORY OF INDIA

Most histories written during al-Biruni's time focused on major events, sultans, and dynasties. Al-Biruni preferred to focus his historical works on culture, religion, and practical information, crafting a more complete account of a time or place. Finished in 1030, al-Biruni's *Tarikh al-Hind* is his most comprehensive work written in this style. The book's title translates to *A History of India*, and although al-Biruni referred to the book as "a simple historic record of facts" in its preface, it stands today as the preeminent reference volume on medieval India. Al-Biruni was able to amass an incredible wealth of information about India during a time when new information did not flow freely out of the country. He is said to have been encouraged to write the treatise by colleagues including Ali Nuh al-Tiflisi, who suggested al-Biruni share his vast knowledge of India and the Hindu people with the rest of the world. Ultimately, al-Biruni brought this knowledge into his overall studies and folded Indian ideas into his search for universal truth.

India included an amazing level of detail and touched on dozens of facets of the Hindu culture. It was the first book to record a complete list of Indian rulers from the pre-Muslim leaders of Kashmir through the then-current rulers of the day; it mapped the positions of towns and described their locations relative to one another; and it illustrated the country's entire western coastline including seaports. In his book, al-Biruni described customs, including marriage, diet, justice, inheritance, and hygiene, and uncovered lesser known subcultures, languages, and scripts. From a social standpoint, he outlined the Indian caste (class) system, and on the topic of religion, he interpreted several passages from the Bhagavad Gita, which is the sacred scripture of Hinduism.

This table of the twelve suns and the names of the months derived from those of the lunar mansions is in an 1159 copy of al-Biruni's *A History of India*. A lunar mansion represents the moon's average daily motion.

Al-Biruni was the first person to introduce the Bhagavad Gita to Muslim readership, and he used it extensively to illustrate similarities and differences between Hindus and Muslims.

He pointed out parallels between the two religions, such as the Hindu belief that ignorance is the bond that ties the soul to this world and that knowledge will serve to gain liberation. This idea is central to Islam as well, and al-Biruni regarded it as the key motivation in his continuous search for universal truth. Conversely, al-Biruni calls out India's caste system as a fundamental contrast between Muslim and Hindu culture. Where Islam recognizes all men as equal, except in piety, the Bhagavad Gita recognizes four distinct social classes. Al-Biruni was a strong opponent of the caste system, describing it in his book as "one set of people treating the others as fools."

German scholar Edward Sachau (1845–1930) first translated *India* into English in the late nineteenth century, and this pioneering book has continued to hold significance across multiple fields of study for almost 1,000 years. Unquestionably al-Biruni's most ambitious work, *India* truly brings together scientific, religious, and cultural disciplines in one united work, and it is perhaps al-Biruni's best effort at applying the concept of al-tawhid. Never losing sight of his virtuous pursuit of truth and unity, and continuing to inspire his fellow Muslims to greatness, al-Biruni closes *India* with the following passage: "We ask God to pardon us for every statement of ours which is not true. We ask Him to lead us to a proper insight into the nature of that which is false and idle that we may sift it so as to distinguish the chaff from the wheat."

TIMELINE

973

Al-Biruni is born near Kath in the kingdom of Khwarizm (present-day Uzbekistan).

990–995

Al-Biruni studies in Kath, Khwarizm, under the patronage of Abu Nasr Mansur ibn Iraq.

995

Al-Biruni completes *Cartography*, a work on the study of charts and maps.

996–997

Al-Biruni goes through a period of instability; studies independently in Rayy without a patron.

998–1004

Al-Biruni studies in Gorgan under the patronage of Shams al-Maali bin Qabus.

1000

Al-Biruni completes his comprehensive history, *The Chronology of Ancient Nations*.

1004–1017

Al-Biruni returns to Khwarizm to study in the court of the Mamunid dynasty.

(continued on following page)

(continued from previous page)

1017

Al-Biruni is taken prisoner by Mahmud Ghaznavi, who invades Khwarizm.

1018–1048

Al-Biruni is forced to study in Ghaznah in the court of the Ghaznavid dynasty.

1020–1029

Al-Biruni embarks upon several research expeditions into India.

1024

Al-Biruni completes his most accurate calculation of Earth's circumference.

1025

Al-Biruni completes his treatise *Book of Coordinates*.

1029

Al-Biruni completes his book *Instruction in the Elements of the Art of Astrology*.

1030

Al-Biruni completes his extensive study of India, *A History of India*.

1048

Al-Biruni dies in Ghaznah.

GLOSSARY

Allah The word used by Arabic-speaking Christians and Muslims to refer to God. Derived from a Semitic root referring to "the divine."

al-tawhid The concept of divine unity that is stressed in Islam. Scholars take from the idea of God's Oneness that all things should be studied holistically.

astrolabe An instrument once used to measure the altitudes of heavenly bodies and to determine their positions and movements.

caliph "Successor to the messenger of God;" the elected head of the Muslim community; regarded as a successor of Muhammad, charged with protecting and upholding Islam.

geocentric Referring to Earth as a center; in astronomy, referring to the medieval notion of Earth at the center of the universe.

geodesy Science of Earth's size and shape; determining the position of points on its surface and dimensions of areas.

heliocentric Referring to the Sun as a center; referring to the modern notion of the Sun at the center of the solar system.

Islam A monotheistic world religion preached by the prophet Muhammad from 610–632; the principal religion of much of Asia and Africa.

mosque A Muslim house of worship, orientated so that the faithful pray facing the holy city of Mecca (Makkah).

Muslim One who follows the religion of Islam, and accepts Muhammad as prophet and the Qur'an as divine revelation.

Qur'an (also Koran) The sacred book of Islam, believed to have been revealed by God in revelations to the prophet Muhammad over the course of about twenty-three years until his death in 632. The word "Qur'an" means recitation.

Sanskrit The language of Hinduism used by the educated classes in India for literary and religious purposes for more than 2,000 years.

sextant A navigational instrument used for measuring the altitudes of celestial bodies to determine latitude and longitude; a successor to the astrolabe.

sultan A ruler of a Muslim territory, usually owing allegiance in principle to the caliph. The title refers to the fact that this ruler commands military power or prestige.

FOR MORE INFORMATION

Arab World and Islamic Resources
P.O. Box 174
Abiquiu, NM 87510
(510) 704-0517
Web site: http://www.awaironline.org

Council on Islamic Education
9300 Gardenia Street, B-3
Fountain Valley, CA 90186
(714) 839-2714
Web site: http://www.cie.org

International Museum of Muslim Cultures
117 East Pascagoula Street
Jackson, MS 39201
(601) 960-0440
Web site: http://www.muslimmuseum.org

The Islamic Information Centre
460 Stapleton Road, Eastville
Bristol BS5 6PA
United Kingdom
(011) 7 902 0037
Web site: http://www.islamicinformationcentre.co.uk

Metropolitan Museum of Art
Islamic Art Division
1000 Fifth Avenue
New York, NY 10028
(212) 535-7710
Web site: http://www.metmuseum.org/Works_Of_Art/
  department.asp?dep=14

WEB SITES

Due to the changing nature of Internet links, the Rosen
Publishing Group, Inc., has developed an online list of Web
sites related to the subject of this book. This site is updated
regularly. Please use this link to access the list:

http://www.rosenlinks.com/gmps/biru

FOR FURTHER READING

Beshore, George. *Science in Early Islamic Culture* (Science of the Past). London, England: Franklin Watts, 1998.

Hayes, John R., ed. *The Genius of Arab Civilization*. 3rd ed. New York, NY: New York University Press, 1992.

Martell, Hazel. *The World of Islam Before 1700* (Looking Back). Orlando, FL: Raintree Pub., 1998.

Menocal, María Rosa. *The Ornament of the World: How Muslims, Jews and Christians Created a Culture of Tolerance in Medieval Spain*. Boston, MA: Little, Brown and Company, 2002.

Swisher, Clarice. *The Spread of Islam* (Turning Points in World History). San Diego, CA: Greenhaven Press, 1998.

BIBLIOGRAPHY

Menocal, María Rosa. *The Ornament of the World: How Muslims, Jews and Christians Created a Culture of Tolerance in Medieval Spain.* Boston, MA: Little, Brown and Company, 2002.

Nasr, Seyyed Hossein. *Abu Rayhan Biruni: Scientist and Scholar Extraordinary.* Tehran, Iran: Ministry of Culture and Arts Press, 1972.

Nasr, Seyyed Hossein. *An Introduction to Islamic Cosmological Doctrines: Conceptions of Nature and Methods Used for Its Study by the Ikhwan al-Safa, al-Biruni, and Ibn Sina.* Boulder, CO: Shambhala Publications, Inc., 1978.

Said, Hakim, and A. Zahid. *Al-Biruni: His Times, Life and Works.* Srinagar, India: Venus Publishing House, 1996.

Sharma, Arvind. *Studies in "Alberuni's India."* Wiesbaden, Germany: Otto Harrassowitz, 1983.

INDEX

About the Author

Bill Scheppler is an award-winning author who has a keen interest in the history and philosophy of the Middle East. He has written on topics such as the war in Iraq and the Guantánamo Bay military tribunals in the wake of the United States' invasion of Afghanistan. Scheppler holds a BA in history and currently resides in the San Francisco Bay area with his wife, Emily.

About the Consultant

Munir A. Shaikh, executive director of the Council on Islamic Education (CIE), reviewed this book. The CIE is a non-advocacy, academic research institute that provides consulting services and academic resources related to teaching about world history and world religions. http://www.cie.org.

Photo Credits

Cover Detail 1973 stamp, Soviet Union; pp. 7, 23 Bildarchiv Preussischer Kulturbesitz/Art Resource, NY; pp. 10–11 Map by Andras Bereznay/http://www.historyonmaps.com; p. 13 © The British Museum/HIP/Art Resource, NY; p. 16 Kunsthistorisches Museum, Vienna, Austria/Bridgeman Art Library; p. 17 © The British Library/Topham-HIP/The Image Works; p. 20 © The British Library: Add. 16561 f.60; p. 26 Detail 1975 stamp, Egypt; p. 29 Used with permission of Edinburgh University Library [Or. Ms 161. f. 162r]; p. 33 Photo and collections of the Bibliothèque Nationale et Universitaire, Strasbourg, MS.4.247, fol. 47a; pp. 34, 62, 86 © Background tiles courtesy of Mosaic House, New York; p. 35 The Pierpont Morgan Library, Ms. M.471, f.330/Art Resource, NY; pp. 37, 40, 50, 85 © The British Library: Or. 8349, photos from Asian and Middle Eastern Division, The New York Public Library, Astor, Lenox and Tilden Foundations; pp. 44, 48, 64, 74, 91, 97, 99 Bibliothèque nationale de France; p. 49 © The British Museum/HIP/The Image Works; p. 52 ©Topham/The Image Works; p. 55 Bridgeman Art Library, London; p. 58 Freer Gallery of Art, Smithsonian Institution, Washington, D.C.: Purchase, F1959.2; p. 61 Museo Real Academia de Medicina, Madrid, Spain, Index/Bridgeman Art Library; p. 66 © The British Library: Or. 12688 f.15v; p. 69 Used with permission of Edinburgh University Library [Or Ms. 20. f. 135r]; p. 70 © Burstein Collection/Corbis; p. 73 The Bodleian Library, University of Oxford, Pococke 400, fol. 12v; p.77 © Ann Ronan Picture Library/HIP/Art Resource, NY; p. 82 © Mary Evans Picture Library/The Image Works; p. 88 © The British Library: Or. 5593 f.6v.

Designer: Les Kanturek; Editor: Kathy Kuhtz Campbell
Photo Researcher: Gabriel Caplan